A Fifth Word and Not co-prod

ALL THE LITTLE LIGHTS

by Jane Upton

All the Little Lights was first performed at
Nottingham Playhouse, on 20 October 2015

ALL THE LITTLE LIGHTS

by Jane Upton

Cast

AMY	Esther-Grace Button
LISA	Sarah Hoare
JOANNE	Tessie Orange-Turner

Artistic, Management and Production Team

Director	Laura Ford
Associate Director	Angharad Jones
Designer	Max Dorey
Lighting Designer	Alexandra Stafford
Sound Designer	Max Pappenheim
Assistant Director	Tilly Branson
Producer	Corinne Salisbury
Associate Producer	Hannah Tookey
Production Managers	Darrell Bracegirdle
	Megan Sheeran
Stage Manager	Sophie Westmoreland

Cast

Esther-Grace Button | Amy

Esther-Grace Button was shortlisted for The Carleton Hobbs Award 2011. Theatre credits include *Sleeping Beauty* (Cast, Doncaster); *Macbeth* (Greenwich); *Fete Or Flight – The Rebels of Newton Wood* (Bush); *As You Like It* (Changeling); *La Ronde* (Tristan Bates); *The Crucible* (Regent's Park Open Air Theatre); *Hansel and Gretel* (Opera North).

Sarah Hoare | Lisa

Sarah Hoare's theatre credits include *'Tis Pity She's a Whore* (Royal Shakespeare Company); *Jerusalem* (Royal Court/Sonia Friedman Productions); *Hag* (The Wrong Crowd); *The Biting Point* (Theatre503). Film credits include *Powder Room*, *Counting Backwards*. Television credits include *Chewing Gum*, *People Just Do Nothing*, *EastEnders*, *Sink or Swim*, *Black Mirror 2*, *Pram Face* and *Some Girls*.

Tessie Orange-Turner | Joanne

Tessie Orange-Turner's theatre credits include *After Orlando* (Finborough); *Sket* (Park); *No Border* (Theatre503); *XY* (Papercut Theatre); *Blister* (Gate); *Bassett* (Soho). Film credits include *You, Me and Him* starring David Tennant, Lucy Punch and Faye Marsay. Television credits include *Casualty*.

Creative Team

Jane Upton | Writer
Jane Upton is currently under commission to Nottingham Playhouse and New Perspectives Theatre Company. Other plays include *Watching the Living*, an adaptation of two Daphne du Maurier short stories (New Perspectives Theatre UK tour, 2014); *Swimming* (Menagerie Theatre Hotbed Festival, 2013/Soho/ Edinburgh Festival, 2014); *Bones* (Fifth Word, Edinburgh Festival/UK tour 2011–2012). Jane has been supported by a bursary from the Peggy Ramsay Foundation. She is also an associate artist with 1623 theatre company.

Laura Ford | Director
Laura Ford is co-founder and Joint Artistic Director of Fifth Word.

Most recent direction for Fifth Word includes *Bones* (Edinburgh Fringe Festival/Tristan Bates/national tour); *Parted Eye* (Q Arts). Rehearsed readings include *Wreck, Still Here* (Nottingham Playhouse); *All The Little Lights* (Derby). Laura regularly works with writers to help develop new plays by directing workshops and showcasing work at different stages.

Angharad Jones | Associate Director
Angharad Jones is co-founder and Joint Artistic Director of Fifth Word.

Directing credits include *Painkillers* (Edinburgh Festival/East Midlands regional tour); *Bones* (Edinburgh Fringe Festival/national tour). Assistant directing credits include *The Trial* (Nottingham Playhouse Young Company). Through developing new work with playwrights, Angharad has jointly directed numerous rehearsed readings including *Wreck* by Toby Campion, recent winner of Fifth Word's Award for Most Promising Playwright.

Max Dorey | Designer
Max Dorey graduated from the Professional Theatre Design MA at Bristol Old Vic Theatre School in 2012. He was a finalist for the Linbury Prize in 2013 and was Assistant Designer at the RSC in 2013/14. In 2016 he was nominated for the UK Theatre Awards Design Award and has been nominated for the Off West End Awards six times.

Set and costume design credits include: *Abigail* (Bunker); *LUV* (Park); *The Collector* (Vaults – nominated for Off West End Award for Best Set Design); *Cargo* (Arcola); *Last of the Boys* (Southwark Playhouse); *After Independence* (Arcola/Papatango); *P'yongyang* (Finborough); *No Villain* (Old Red Lion/Trafalgar Studios – nominated for Off West End Award for Best Set Design); *All The Little Lights* (Fifth Word); *And Then Come The Nightjars* (Theatre503/Bristol Old Vic/UK tour – nominated for a 2016 UK Theatre Award for Best Design); *Orson's Shadow* (Southwark Playhouse); *Teddy* (Southwark Playhouse – nominated for Off West End Award for Best Set Design); *Lardo, Marching On Together* (Old Red Lion); *Coolatully* (Finborough); *Sleight and Hand* (Edinburgh Fringe); *I Can Hear You, This Is Not An Exit* (The Other Place at the Courtyard, RSC/Royal Court Upstairs); *Black Jesus* (Finborough); *The Duke in Darkness* (Tabard – nominated for Off West End Award for Best Set Design); *Marguerite* (Tabard – nominated for Off West End Award for Best Set Design).

Alexandra Stafford | Lighting Designer

Alexandra Stafford is delighted to be working again with Fifth Word on *All The Little Lights* having previously lit the UK tour of *Amateur Girl*.

Recent theatre credits include *Sherlock Holmes & The Hound of the Baskervilles*, *Betrayal* (York Theatre Royal); *The Season Ticket* (Northern Stage/Pilot); *Outsiders*, *Antigone* (Pilot/UK tour); *Around the World in 80 Days* (The New Vic/Royal Exchange); *The Remarkable Tale of Oliver Twist*, *Emil & The Detectives* (Red Earth); *Sleuth*, *Posh*, *Private Lives* (Nottingham Playhouse); *The Kreutzer Sonata* (Chipping Norton/Arcola); *Stones In His Pockets* (Dukes Lancaster/Chipping Norton); *Così fan tutte*, *Hansel & Gretel* (Clonter Opera) and eleven pantomimes for Harrogate Theatre, the most recent being *Dick Whittington*.

Alex was the Head of Lighting at Derby Playhouse from 1999 until 2003. Lighting designs for Derby Playhouse include *My Dad's Corner Shop*, *Educating Rita*, *Up 'n' Under*, *The Blue Room*, *Bouncers*, *Three Viewings*, *A Life in the Theatre*, *A Slice of Saturday Night* and ten pantomimes.

Max Pappenheim | Sound Designer

Max Pappenheim's theatre credits include *The Children* (Royal Court); *Sex With Strangers*, *Labyrinth* (Hampstead); *Ophelias Zimmer* (Schaubühne, Berlin/Royal Court); *Sheppey*, *Blue/Heart*, *Little Light*, *The Distance* (Orange Tree, Richmond); *The Gaul* (Hull Truck); *Toast* (Park/59E59 Theatres, New York); *Jane Wenham* (Out of Joint); *Waiting for Godot* (Sheffield Crucible); *My Eyes Went Dark* (Traverse, Edinburgh); *Cargo* (Arcola); *Commonwealth* (Almeida); *A Lovely Sunday For Creve Coeur* (Print Room); *WINK* (Theatre503); *Fabric*, *Invincible* (national tours); *Spamalot*, *The Glass Menagerie*, *Strangers on a Train* (English Theatre, Frankfurt); *Kiki's Delivery Service*, *Johnny Got His Gun*, *Three Sisters*, *Fiji Land*, *Our Ajax* (Southwark Playhouse); *Mrs Lowry and Son* (Trafalgar Studios); *Martine*, *Black Jesus*, *Somersaults*, *The Fear of Breathing* (Finborough); The Faction's Rep season 2015 (New Diorama); *Shopera: Carmen* (Royal Opera House); *The Hotel Plays* (Langham Hotel).

As Associate: *The Island* (Young Vic); *Fleabag* (Soho). Max is an Associate Artist of The Faction.

Radio includes *Home Front* (BBC Radio 4).

Tilly Branson | Assistant Director

Tilly Branson is a director and dramaturg with a particular interest in new writing and women's voices. Past work includes *Getting Better Slowly* by Nick Wood (Lincoln Drill Hall/national tour 2016–2017); *Think of England* by Madeleine Gould for Anonymous is a Woman (national tour 2016); *Acting Alone* by Ava Hunt (international tour 2015–16); *Man to Man* by Manfred Karge (Mercury Colchester 2013/Park, London 2014); *Entertaining Angels* by Brendan Murray (New Perspectives, rural tour 2013); *End To End* (The Gramophones, Edinburgh Fringe/national tour 2013–2015). She regularly works with writers on scripts in development and has directed several rehearsed readings and showcases of new writing. She has recently completed an AHRC funded PhD researching the UK rural touring sector.

About Fifth Word

Fifth Word is run by joint artistic directors Laura Ford and Angharad Jones and is an associate company at Nottingham Playhouse.

We produce and tour ambitious new plays from the most exciting voices around the UK, shining a light on unheard stories and bringing fresh, engaging work to theatres and audiences nationwide.

'Observations of the dehumanising influence of the sex industry do not come much sharper' ★ ★ ★ ★ *Guardian* on *Amateur Girl*

We present new plays that entertain, emotionally engage, and spark debate relevant to our times. Located in the East Midlands, we nurture regional voices and the next generation of playwriting talent. Fifth Word held their inaugural award for Most Promising Playwright in partnership with Nottingham Playhouse in 2015.

'Storytelling to perfection... shockingly realistic. Left me agape in wide-eyed awe' ★ ★ ★ ★ ★ *Three Weeks* on *Bones*

Fifth Word's most recent productions include: *Bones* by Jane Upton (Edinburgh Festival, 2011, UK tour, 2012), *Amateur Girl* by Amanda Whittington (UK tour 2014).

Rehearsed readings: *All The Little Lights* (Derby Theatre 2014), *Still Here* (Nottingham Playhouse 2015) and *Wreck* (Nottingham Playhouse 2015).

'Expertly Crafted' ★ ★ ★ ★ *The Times* on *Amateur Girl*

Fifth Word is a previous winner of the Olwen Wymark Theatre Encouragement Award.

'Winning the Encouragement Award for developing new writing, from the Writer's Guild of Great Britain, gave Fifth Word national recognition. Its nurturing of this play is exemplary' *The Stage* on *Bones*

About Nottingham Playhouse

Nottingham Playhouse has been one of the UK's leading producing theatres since its foundation in 1948. It welcomes over 110,000 customers through its doors each year and creates productions large and small from timeless classics and enthralling family shows to adventurous new commissions, often touring work nationally and internationally.

Notable productions include *1984* – three runs in the West End and currently on tour in Australia; *Any Means Necessary*, a new play about undercover policing; *Tony's Last Tape* which toured nationally last year; a forthcoming revival of *Touched* starring BAFTA-winning actress Vicky McClure and Aisling Loftus, and a production of *The Kite Runner* which is currently on at the West End's Wyndham's Theatre.

www.nottinghamplayhouse.co.uk

Artistic Director: Giles Croft
Chief Executive: Stephanie Sirr
Artistic Director Designate: Adam Penford

Acknowledgements

Fifth Word would like to thank:

Kate Chapman, Esther Richardson, Sarah Brigham, Derby Theatre, Safe & Sound, Natalie Ibu, Sooki McShane, Nic Wass, James Grieve, Rob Drummer, Ben Monks, Will Young, Corinne Salisbury, Giles Croft, Fiona Buffini and Nottingham Playhouse.

A special thank you to Jane Upton for giving us the opportunity to share these girls' stories. And for her patience and perseverance throughout the development of this play.

Fifth Word gratefully acknowledges the support received from:

Arts Council England, Nottingham Playhouse, Derby Theatre, and the Unity Theatre Trust.

ALL THE LITTLE LIGHTS

Jane Upton

Acknowledgements

I'm very grateful to the following people:

Amie Burns Walker, Nadia Clifford, Darren Daly, Katie Elin-Salt, Sarah Hoare, Abigail Hood and Rosie Wyatt for their energy, ideas and fearlessness when workshopping early drafts.

Kate Chapman and Esther Richardson for their sharp dramaturgical insight and guidance and for always inspiring me.

Sarah Brigham and Derby Theatre, and Giles Croft, Fiona Buffini and Nottingham Playhouse for their valuable support during various stages of this process.

Nicola Dalby and colleagues at Safe & Sound for being open, insightful and generous with their time and support, and for all they do for us as a society. And to Adam Buss at Derby Quad for introducing us.

Stephen Jeffreys and Lloyd Trott at RADA for teaching me some really helpful lessons between drafts.

Micheline Steinberg for her support and guidance and for answering my endless emails.

Neville and Sheila Aitchison for letting me cry in their spare bed.

Robert, Jennifer, Katie and Jonathan Upton for their continued love, support and inspiration.

And special thanks to Laura Ford and Angharad Jones who always believed in this play and were tenacious in its development. I've loved learning with you.

J.U.

For Mark and Edith

4

Characters

AMY, *twelve*
JOANNE, *sixteen*
LISA, *fifteen*

Note on Text

Words in brackets should not be spoken.

A forward slash (/) marks a point of interruption or an overlap in dialogue.

A larger gap between lines suggests a pause, a rest, a breath, a few beats. To be decided.

On page 11 Lisa gives her year of birth. This can be changed according to when the play is performed to make mathematical sense.

When a line ends without punctuation, the next line should follow closely without interrupting.

This text went to press before the end of rehearsals and so may differ slightly from the play as performed.

Note on Time

Although the play is set in September, for the 2017 UK tour dates between February and May, we changed the setting to February to make it more immediate and to make sense of the simple mathematics on page 11. This meant slight alterations to the text, as follows:

Page 7:

JOANNE. Didn't forget, see. I always remember. September. All the clever ones are born in September.

Was changed to:

JOANNE. Didn't forget, see. February. I always remember.

Page 43:

JOANNE. I was in there yesterday. Sat in our seats. Just me. They still do them cookies you like. They're pumpkins at the minute. Cos Hallowe'en and that.

Was changed to:

JOANNE. I was in there yesterday. Sat in our seats. Just me. They still do them cookies you like. They're hearts at the minute. Cos Valentine's and that.

Obviously this also changes the way the play is performed. It is colder and darker, and February, trapped between winter and spring, goes hand in hand with the wasteland setting. It brings a different quality to the play.

For future productions, the play should either be set in September or February; never spring or summer.

Preset

Dusk.

Somewhere on the outskirts of an urban sprawl, high up overlooking houses, next to a railway line.

AMY *and* JOANNE *are putting up a tent. They set up a little camping stove.* JOANNE *lays out a tea towel, a Kellogg's Variety Pack and a cheap bottle of vodka.*

This is done as the audience is entering and being seated. It doesn't matter if they don't see it all.

As the space is set, there is the sound of a train in the distance. It gets closer and closer. As the sound reaches a crescendo the lights go out.

LISA. I can't stay.

JOANNE. You just got here.

LISA. I know / but

JOANNE. Happy birthday!

LISA. Thanks.

JOANNE. Didn't forget, see. I always remember. September.
All the clever ones are born in September.

D'ya want a / drink?

LISA. I can't.

JOANNE. Come on, just one

LISA. I've got to / go

JOANNE. You just got here. Why d'ya come if you're not
gonna stay for a drink?

LISA. Cos you said you were gonna burn Pam's face off with a
bottle of acid

JOANNE. Oh come on. I had to get you here somehow, though.
Din't I, though?
Come on.
Done all this. For your birthday.

JOANNE *pulls a bottle from her pocket and holds it up.*

Look. It's not even acid. It's water.

It is.

I / swear

LISA. Drink it then.

JOANNE. What?

LISA. Drink it. If it's water.

JOANNE. I hate water.

LISA. Drink it.

> / If it's not acid, drink it.

JOANNE. I don't like water.

> JOANNE *stares at* LISA *for a few seconds.* LISA *stares back.*

> JOANNE *slowly raises the bottle to her lips and takes a mouthful. She starts to choke.*

LISA. What the… Joanne, pack it up, stop it, stop it!

> JOANNE *spits the water out of her mouth like a fountain.*

JOANNE. Fucking hate water.

LISA. Twat!

JOANNE. What you done to your hair anyway?

LISA. Just dyed it. Had it cut.

JOANNE. Looks like Harry Potter.

LISA. Cheers.

JOANNE. Joke. I'm joking.

> I liked it long. But.

LISA. Can do loads with it.

JOANNE. Really?

LISA. Yeah – like quiffs and I can pin it and stuff.

> Usually just wear it like this though, so.

JOANNE. Makes you look older.

LISA. Yeah.

JOANNE. So you're not into girls then?

LISA. What?

JOANNE. What? Just, cos the short hair and the / hoody and

LISA. Shut up.

JOANNE. What? Fucking 'ell. Sorry. It's just, a bit…

> AMY *comes on carrying a few sticks*. LISA *is startled at first*.

> That ain't gonna make a fire!

AMY. I couldn't find any.

JOANNE. They're all wet. You can't use wet sticks. Seen it on *Bear Grylls*.

> Amy. Lisa. Lisa. Amy.

AMY. Hiya. Happy birthday.

LISA. Cheers.

AMY. Your hair's different.

JOANNE. She's seen pictures.

AMY. S'nice.

JOANNE. Amy's idea to go camping. She's been before.

LISA. How d'ya know each other?

JOANNE. Mates.

LISA. From where?

JOANNE. Where was it, Amy?

AMY. That twitchel. You was there. You was up on that wall.

JOANNE. Oh yeah. She'd been beat up.

LISA. Who by?

AMY. Sarah Shaw. She took her dog to school in a bag.

JOANNE. It's a fucking Alsatian as well.

AMY. Joanne come into school and sorted her out.

JOANNE. What did I say?

AMY. She said 'touch her again and I'll cut your eyes out / and feed 'em to your dog in a bag'

JOANNE. feed 'em to your fucking dog in a bag.

AMY. She's in love with her dog.

JOANNE. Seen her wanking it off in the back row of the
Odeon, didn't we?

AMY. Yeah.

JOANNE. Seen her rubbing Marmite all up her cunt and letting
her dog lick it out.
Seen her fucking breastfeeding it in the Asda café.

LISA. Why'd she beat you up?

JOANNE. Didn't have no mates, did you?

AMY. And my nana's got a baby.

LISA. What?

JOANNE. She lives with her nana, who's, get this, got a baby.
(*Sings.*) With your wrinkled pussy, you can be my lover.

LISA. How old?

JOANNE. Old.

The baby's massive as well, innit? Like they feed it on
fucking pizzas.

LISA. You seen it?

JOANNE. Yeah, you brung it out a couple of times didn't you?

AMY. Yeah. We babysat.

JOANNE. We babysat her auntie. That's what it is, innit?
Fucking weird.
Fat little fucker. Like it's made of playdough.

AMY. Sarah Shaw seen us, at the petrol station. She just walked
past. Didn't even look up.

JOANNE. Alright now, aren't you? At school and that?

AMY. Yeah.

JOANNE. When she goes!

AMY *and* JOANNE *laugh*.

What we gonna do about a fire?

AMY. We could use a sleeping bag. Sometimes you use the bit
inside a sleeping bag. There's a woman off the Olympics,
she used her sleeping bag and Bear Grylls said it was good.

JOANNE. Were you watching that with me?

AMY. Yeah.

JOANNE. Fucking loves her TV, this one. Square eyes, aren't
you? She should be on *Gogglebox*. Always chatting shit
aren't you? Sometimes she says something and I'm like 'that
is pure *Gogglebox*'.
We ain't using the sleeping bags.

AMY. How old are you? Today?

LISA. Ain't my birthday today.

JOANNE. It is.

LISA. 15th.

JOANNE. Thought it was 19th.

LISA. Nah.

JOANNE. Since when?

LISA. Since I was born. 2000.

AMY. So how old are you?

JOANNE. Work it out.

AMY. I'm rubbish at maths.

JOANNE. What year is it now? Work it out.

AMY. Nana said they dropped me on my head when I was
a baby.

LISA. Fifteen. How old are you?

AMY. Twelve.

LISA. Year 8?

AMY. Yeah. When I go.

    AMY *looks at* JOANNE *for a laugh.* JOANNE *ignores her.*

JOANNE. Doesn't matter though, does it? What? Four days late.
Still celebrating. Haven't seen you for, how long's it been?

AMY. Joanne's got you loads of things.

LISA. What?

AMY. Can we give her the presents?

JOANNE. Not yet.

JOANNE *hands drinks to* AMY *and* LISA.

LISA. I don't want any presents. (*About the drink.*) What is it?

JOANNE. Cocktail. Well, mainly just vodka. And a bit of rain water.

LISA. I'm alright.

JOANNE. Just hold it. You might want it.

JOANNE *picks up the Variety Pack.*

I've got you these, for the morning.

AMY. Shotgun Coco Pops.

JOANNE. Lisa's having the Coco Pops. You can have the Cornflakes.

LISA. I'm not staying.

JOANNE. Just tonight. For the party.

LISA. No way.

JOANNE. Just us three.

Vodka, music, we've got a stove, look. Proper. Works and that.

AMY. Presents.

JOANNE. Spaghetti Hoops. Your favourite.

LISA. Haven't had 'em for ages.

JOANNE. Used to be.

LISA. S'getting dark.

AMY. That light comes on. When it gets dark. Security light. So no snakes can get in the tent.

JOANNE. Ain't no snakes up here.

LISA. They'll be wondering where / I am

JOANNE. You're allowed out for one night.

LISA. I can't just disappear. They'll come looking.

JOANNE. I couldn't live like it. All the fucking rules / and

LISA. It's alright.

They're nice.

AMY *has gone over to the tent. She pulls out a birthday cake.*

AMY. We got you a birthday cake. Candles, look. We can light them. We've got a lighter.

JOANNE. Fuckin 'ell, Amy, that's for later, that's meant to be a / surprise

AMY. I thought it might make her / stay, you want her to

JOANNE. Put it away. Fuck's sake. She's not staying.

AMY *puts it away quietly.*

LISA. It's nice. Cheers.

JOANNE. Everything's nice these days.

AMY. We didn't make it. We just bought it. From Tescos. There was some like caterpillars and one that had Peppa Pig on it but we thought that was for babies.

JOANNE. So what's it like? At the new place?

LISA. Ni... Alright.

JOANNE. You got your own room?

LISA. Yeah.

JOANNE. Big?

LISA. Not really.

Pete plays guitar. Pam's husband.

JOANNE. Pete? Like –

LISA. A different Pete.

JOANNE. Yeah, but, is he like –

LISA. No.

JOANNE. Cos you wonder don't you. These blokes who want other people's kids to come and live in their houses. Just seems fucking dirty really, dunnit?

LISA. He's not.

JOANNE. What so he just starts playing guitar all of a sudden like some fucking hippy?

LISA. We all sit round and he sings.

JOANNE. Sings what?

LISA. Old stuff.

JOANNE. What like fucking Beethoven or something?

LISA. Beatles I think. Not really sure.

JOANNE. Sing it.

LISA. Don't know it.

>   AMY *sings the first line of 'Eleanor Rigby' by Lennon-McCartney, getting the words a bit wrong.*

AMY. Eleanor Rigby, sits in the church where her wedding has been…

LISA. Yeah. Like that.

JOANNE. How do you know that?

AMY. Nana's old boyfriend was in a band at The Royal Oak. Used to get sips of his beer. Got dead pissed.

JOANNE. On a few sips?

AMY. Used to get like half a pint.

JOANNE. Half a pint of beer? Fucking 'ell!

>   (*To* LISA.) What do you do, when Pete starts doing that hippy shit?

LISA. Dunno, just sort of look down I s'pose. Pam closes her eyes and just like

JOANNE. What?

LISA. Sort of sways.

JOANNE. Fucking 'ell you're in a cult.

>   Is it just you, living there? Kids, like?

LISA. Yeah.

JOANNE. Intense.

Have some Hoops.

LISA. No one's coming are they?

JOANNE. Like who?

LISA. Alright.

JOANNE. What?

LISA. I'll have some.

JOANNE. Please.

LISA. But then I've got to go.

JOANNE. Course.

> JOANNE *goes over to the stove and puts a pan of Spaghetti Hoops on.*

LISA. My feet are frozen.

JOANNE. Fucking love that film.

AMY. We watched it the other day, din't we?

They was showing it on Saturday morning cinema club.

JOANNE (*to* LISA). You seen it?

LISA. *Frozen*? Yeah. We watched it, din't we? At Showcase.

JOANNE. Did we?

LISA. Ages ago.

AMY. We watched *Tangled* as well.

JOANNE (*to* AMY). Pretended to be your big sister, didn't I? Cos you gotta be with someone sixteen or over. Saw *Snow White* as well. *Witches*, wannit? (*In voice of Head Witch.*) 'Ladies, remove your wigs!' *E.T.* (*In voice of E.T.*) 'Ell-i-ott.'

AMY (*in voice of E.T.*). 'Ell-i-ott. Home.'

JOANNE. She cried all the way through it, din't ya, Amy? Fucking retard.

AMY. Yeah but E.T.'s like in this bag and he's all white and Elliott thinks he's dead. I thought he was dead! And he has to leave his friends, at the end. He doesn't want to. (*In voice of E.T.*) 'Ell-i-ott.'

JOANNE. Two quid a ticket. You'll have to come one time. She cried all the way through *Frozen* as well.

AMY. Yeah but it's well sad cos their mum and dad die on this boat in this storm and Elsa's got these ice powers.

LISA. I've seen it.

AMY. And then Anna's like – (*In childlike American accent.*) 'Let's build a snowman.' But she's on her own at the door, Elsa won't come out cos she doesn't want to hurt her sister with her ice powers.

JOANNE. Soft as shit, this one.

AMY. *E.T.*'s the best though.

JOANNE. Do that thing, Amy.

AMY. What thing?

JOANNE. With your top. E.T.

AMY. Oh yeah.

> AMY *starts to pull her top up from the back so her head is poking through the neck hole.*

JOANNE. Entertainment for the party. Fucking breaks me, this. Well funny.

AMY. (*E.T. voice*). Ell-i-ott.

JOANNE. That's not it. Put your shoes on, like you did; do it like... fucking cracks me up.

> AMY *starts to take her shoes off.*

(*To* LISA.) There's this bit, right, where E.T.'s dressed like an old woman and he hides in the toys and... Oh, put the music on, Amy. Y'know, the E.T. music. Get it on your phone.

AMY. Oh yeah!

> AMY *fumbles to get her phone out.*

Joanne give me her old phone. It's an iPhone.

AMY *starts to search for the music on her phone. At the same time* JOANNE *gets her phone out and starts calling* AMY.

JOANNE. She had a right piece of shit before. Couldn't even take pictures.

AMY*'s phone starts playing a popular contemporary track.*

AMY. Hey!

Plays our favourite song when she rings me.

So I know it's her.

JOANNE *ends call. Music stops.*

And her face pops up.

JOANNE. Hurry up then.

AMY. You're putting me off. Wait. Okay. Ready.
You be the spaceship.

JOANNE. Fuck off. I'm Elliott.

AMY. Just for this bit.

JOANNE. Lisa, you be spaceship.

LISA. What?

JOANNE. Use this torch. Hold it up. That's it.

LISA *holds the torch limply.* AMY *kneels in front of* LISA. *She puts her knees into her shoes. She puts her arms in her sleeves and her head is poking out of her top. She is in full E.T. character.*

JOANNE *backs up a bit.*

JOANNE. Okay, I'm Elliott. It's the bit where he's going. Where E.T.'s going back to Mars or whatever. Yeah?

AMY. Yeah.

JOANNE. Start the music then.

AMY *starts the* E.T. *theme music on her phone.*

Fucking love this music.

JOANNE *starts to walk towards the spaceship as Elliott.*

AMY (*as E.T.*). Come.

JOANNE (*as Elliott*). Stay.

> *As E.T.,* AMY *lifts her arm and a stick she gathered earlier emerges from her sleeve as a long E.T. finger. She touches her lips then her heart.*

AMY (*as E.T.*). Ouch.

> JOANNE *repeats the action as Elliott.*

JOANNE (*as Elliott*). Ouch.

> AMY *leans in to hug* JOANNE – *probably her legs.*

What you doing?

AMY. They hug at this bit.

JOANNE. Do the next bit then.

AMY. You've got to kneel down.

JOANNE. Fuck's sake. (*Kneels down.*) Music goes mad now. You listening, Lise?

LISA. Yeah.

AMY (*as E.T. – putting a twig finger to Elliott's head*). I'll be – [right here]

> *The music buffers at the climax.* LISA *isn't watching. She's checking her phone.*

Sorry. Wait. Wait.

JOANNE. Fuck's sake.

> AMY *messes with her phone, music comes back.*

AMY. Okay. (*As E.T.*) I'll be right – [here]

> *The music buffers.* LISA *isn't paying attention.* JOANNE *knocks the twig finger out of* AMY*'s hand.*

JOANNE. Forget it.

AMY. I can do it.

JOANNE. Shouldn't've give you the phone if you can't even work it.

AMY. I can. Wait.

Music comes back on.

JOANNE. Leave it, Amy.

Music buffers again then comes back on.

Leave it! Fuck's sake!

Music stops.

Slowly AMY *rids herself of E.T., dropping the twig finger to the floor, emerging from the hoody and putting her shoes back on.*

JOANNE *puts the Spaghetti Hoops into plastic party bowls like at a kids' party.*

Did Pam and Pete give you a party, did they?

LISA. Yeah.

JOANNE. What was it?

LISA. We went Nando's.

JOANNE. Quarter chicken mild, chips, coleslaw, thank you! S'what I always have. Go sometimes. Quite often.

LISA. She'd made me a cake. They put it in the back then the waiter came out with it and everyone was singing. Like almost the whole restaurant was singing.

JOANNE. Not really a restaurant is it? S'not fucking Gordon Ramsey.

JOANNE *is getting little paper hats out of her bag, ignoring* LISA.

Hang on. Got these.

LISA. It was proper embarrassing.

JOANNE *gives party hats to* LISA *and* AMY. AMY *puts hers on.*

JOANNE. Put one on. And look.

JOANNE *opens a rucksack and a helium balloon on a weight floats out and stops.*

Good innit?

LISA. Yeah.

LISA *is holding her party hat.*

JOANNE. Put it on.

LISA *doesn't put the hat on. Neither does* JOANNE.

AMY (*about the balloon – with her mouth full*). They're well expensive. I got one in Wales once. Had to use all my spending money.

JOANNE. Ah God, you're right, Lise. Spaghetti Hoops are fucking awesome, aren't they?

LISA. Yeah.

AMY *is putting a Spaghetti Hoop on her ring finger. She's got tomato sauce everywhere.*

AMY. Look, I'm married.

JOANNE. Who to?

AMY. 'S a secret. Would you rather marry a spider or kiss a frog?

JOANNE. Fucking 'ell.
Kiss a frog.

AMY. Yeah but if you kiss a frog you might get diseases. Marry a spider then you can stamp on it after the wedding.

JOANNE. No cos all its spider friends would come and fuck you up for murdering their mate.

AMY. Spiders don't work like that. That's ants. And bees. Did it at school.

JOANNE. Do you ever shut up?

AMY. Yeah, sometimes. Sometimes I'm just like quiet for ages, just looking at the wall, thinking, or sometimes on the bus I'm quiet, cos I'm on my own, some people sit on their own and still chat shit but I just don't speak. At all. For ages.

JOANNE. You pissed?

AMY. No.
Bit.

JOANNE. Good girl. Have some more.

It is *nice* though, innit?

LISA. What?

JOANNE. Being up here. On our own. Just us.

AMY. Yeah.

JOANNE. Lise?

LISA. What?

Sound of a train coming.

JOANNE. Hear that?

LISA. Yeah.

AMY. What?

JOANNE. Train! Come on!

JOANNE runs up towards the railway tracks. LISA hesitates. AMY doesn't know what's happening.

Come on, Lisa. First one to jump off's a wet pussy.

Suddenly LISA runs and takes over JOANNE. AMY follows behind. They run through the fence and up on to the railway track.

AMY. What we doing?

LISA. Gotta stay on. Long as you dare.

JOANNE. We always used to do this. Used to do it all the time.

LISA. Feet are buzzing.

AMY. Like pins and needles. Like… arrgh. It's in my knees.

JOANNE. Like them kids in *Witches*, turning to mice.

AMY (*like the kids in* The Witches). Arrrrrgh!

JOANNE (*like the kids in* The Witches) Arrrrrgh!

LISA. Feels like you're on fire! Like every bit of you's electric!

JOANNE. It's there. / Can you see it?

LISA. Like sparks are gonna shoot out of you.

AMY. It's getting / close.

LISA. Light you up.

AMY. I can see it. It's dead close.

> LISA *lets out a big sound, like she's free for a few seconds.*

JOANNE. Don't jump. Don't you dare fucking jump, / Amy.

AMY. I won't. I won't.

JOANNE. I mean it. Don't you dare.

> JOANNE *holds* AMY*'s arm so she can't jump.*

Don't you fucking…

Jump off together. Ready?

One…

ALL. Two…

> JUMP!!!

> *The train crashes past. The girls laugh and squeal.*
> JOANNE *is watching* LISA *who is moved by the experience.*
> AMY *looks half-terrified, half-amazed.*

AMY. Fucking 'ell! Fuck-ing hell!

> *They stay up near the track. They get their breath back.*

> *They look out over the town. It's peaceful.*

> JOANNE *points to one of the houses.*

Lisa, who lives there d'ya reckon?

LISA. What? Ah, no.

JOANNE. What d'ya mean, no? Y'used to fucking love that game.

> (*To* AMY.) She's amazing at it. Comes out with some right stuff. (*Pointing again.*) That one, Lise.

LISA. Nah.

JOANNE (*to* AMY). Never heard no one come out with shit like her. Not like a real-life person.

AMY. What d'ya have to do?

JOANNE. Nah, it's Lisa's game. (*Pointing again.*) Go on, Lise, who lives there d'ya reckon?

The big one, with six windows.

LISA. Sidney and Camille.

JOANNE. Fucking 'ell!

See what I mean?

Where d'ya even get it from?

LISA. He's like a captain in the army. And she's got really white tits.

He fucks her in the kitchen, but he makes her sit on a chopping board, and then he cleans it with bleach.

JOANNE. Mentalist. What about that one?

LISA. Which one?

JOANNE. With the weird little garden.

AMY. Joanne and Amy.

LISA. Bob and Sandra.

JOANNE. Bob and Sandra.

LISA. She's got big hair, like Amy Winehouse-type hair, only it's yellow. She keeps little birds in it, budgies, and photos of her long-lost kids.

JOANNE. Where are they?

LISA. Bob got jealous so he put them on a one-way ferry to a country he'd never heard of.

JOANNE. What's he like? Bob.

LISA. He's got spit in his mouth.

AMY. Everyone's got spit in their mouth.

LISA. Yeah but he's got too much, so you can see it in the corners, know what I mean?

JOANNE. Ah yeah. So it trickles everywhere when he goes down on you.

AMY. Gross.

JOANNE. Look dead cosy, don't they? All the little lights.

S'a trick though. Same shit in every one.

Houses full of Keep Calm and Drink Your Fucking Tea.

LISA. Pam's got that sign. In the kitchen.

JOANNE. Sounds the sort.

LISA. Not the 'fucking' bit. But…

It is a bit weird.

JOANNE. What?

LISA. When he plays guitar.

JOANNE. D'ya want some more Hoops? There's loads. They're cold / but

JOANNE *gets* LISA *some more Spaghetti Hoops.*

LISA. I'm alright

JOANNE. Can heat 'em up.

LISA. I'm full.

AMY. I'll have some.

JOANNE. Cake then? Light the candles, Amy.

AMY. Ah yeah!

AMY *goes into the tent and starts putting candles in the cake.*

LISA. I'm alright. I'm full.

JOANNE. Always room for cake though, int there. Bet you wasn't too full after your Nando's was you? Sorry I didn't make you a cake but I ain't exactly got the facilities, have I?

LISA. You still there?

JOANNE. Yeah. In case you were wondering.

LISA. I was.

JOANNE. You didn't ask.

Why didn't you tell me where you were living?

LISA. Didn't think you'd want to know, after / the

JOANNE. You left loads of stuff at the house.
All that make-up we got.

I chucked it away.

I burnt it actually.

I give that Topshop dress to Amy.

'Happy Birthday' by Stevie Wonder starts playing on AMY*'s phone. She appears from the tent clutching her phone and the cake with lit candles. She starts wobbly-walking towards them.*

The music buffers then carries on.

LISA *tries to blow out the candles. They relight. She tries again. They relight.* AMY *is stifling laughter, as if she knows something hilarious.*

AMY. S'them magic candles. They never go out. I had 'em for my birthday. Look, they never go out.

I got 'em on purpose, Joanne.

AMY *starts blowing them. She is being over the top, childlike and giddy.*

Look. You think they're out, then they come back again.
Look! Like magic.

The music buffers then starts again. AMY *is still giddy.*

How do they do it? Look. Can't blow 'em out. Look.

JOANNE *gets the bottle of water from her pocket and pours it over the candles. Music buffers and stops.*

What you doing?

JOANNE. Shit cake anyway.

AMY. I'm starving.

JOANNE. You ain't starving. Shovelled a tray of chips down you before we came.

LISA. From the chippy?

JOANNE. Course from the chippy.

AMY. Have you been?

LISA. Yeah.

AMY. We could go later.

JOANNE. Not if you're gonna act like that. Like a fucking baby on acid. Showing me up.

AMY. TJ said 'come back any time'.

He winked at me.

JOANNE. Yeah.

Cos he likes you.

AMY. Does he?

JOANNE. Getting on my nerves, always going on about you?

AMY. Me?

JOANNE. Yeah, you.

AMY. What's he say?

JOANNE. Says he thinks you're cute. But not like a baby cute.

Says he likes it when you wear your hair up.

AMY. Shut up.

JOANNE. What? He did. D'ya think he's fit?

AMY. He's well old.

JOANNE. Thirty-nine.

AMY. Is he?

JOANNE. Knows what he's doing.
Lisa's kissed him.

AMY (*to* LISA). Have you?

JOANNE. Yeah.

AMY. What was it like?

JOANNE. Good, wannit, Lise?

LISA. Yeah.

AMY. I dunno.

JOANNE. D'ya fancy someone at school or summat?

AMY. They're all babies at school.

JOANNE. Exactly. TJ said you seem dead mature.

AMY. Did he?

JOANNE. Yeah, he did.
Han't seen you going retarded over magic fucking candles though, has he? Give her a present.

AMY. Can I?

JOANNE. Yeah.

AMY *gets a present out of the tent. It's wrapped up in cheap kids' paper. She gives it to* LISA.

LISA. I don't / want

JOANNE. Open it.

LISA *starts opening the present.*

You're welcome.

LISA. Thanks.

AMY. We chose it. We both did. We looked all around for ages. And Joanne said we could get it, cos she's got the money.

LISA *holds it up. It's a* Frozen *onesie.*

For tonight. So you're not cold in the tent.

LISA. I'm not / staying

JOANNE. Yeah but, for a bit… put it on, come on. You look a bit like Anna [from *Frozen*]. You did. Before you cut your hair. But you could get a wig.

LISA. What?

JOANNE. Be one of them people who dresses up in Disney. Get paid loads. You don't have to look that much like 'em. You just join this website.
Remember Sharon?

LISA. Yeah, course.

JOANNE. She does it. Dresses up as Elsa.

LISA. Sharon?

JOANNE. Yeah. Cos she dyed her hair bright white, din't she? Used to get me combing all the knots out. Gets dead tangled when you bleach it.

AMY (*laughing*). *Tangled*. We watched that, din't we?

JOANNE. Yeah.

LISA. Where's she do it?

JOANNE. Just in the bath. I helped her.

LISA. No. The Elsa thing. Disney World?

JOANNE. Disney World? Yeah, yeah. Disney World Florida. No. Skegness. She moved there. Always wanted to live by the sea. Walks round the streets meeting kids, letting 'em take selfies with her and that. Gets twenty-five quid an hour. Does it four hours a day then puts her jeans on and eats candy floss.

LISA. How d'ya know?

JOANNE. Went visiting her, din't I? Everyone still thinks we're sisters. (*To* AMY.) She tells everyone. Took me to Asda once to get some trainers. I was trying 'em on, fucking shit they were, looking back. I was trying 'em on and the woman goes 'is this your sister' and Sharon goes 'yeah'. Like that. Didn't miss a heartbeat.

(*To* LISA.) We could go. Visit her. She's got this room. Covered her bed in toys she won on the grabbers. She gets loads of money for the arcade. She's making loads.

LISA. I thought she was a cleaner. At the B&Bs.

JOANNE. Nah.

LISA. She cleaned everything up. After. Cos she was too old.

AMY. Too old for what?

JOANNE. Waitressing.
Nah, she left that.

LISA. Left?

JOANNE. Yeah.

LISA. What did you do?

JOANNE. Me? Nothing.

LISA. Did she tell you?

JOANNE. What?

LISA. That she was going?

JOANNE. She tried but, I was out, wan't I?

LISA. Thought she'd tell you.

JOANNE. Why?

LISA. Cos she's like your big sister.

JOANNE. No she didn't tell me. Don't expect her to. Why the
fuck would she?

LISA. Thought she'd say.

JOANNE. Like you, you mean?

Skegness is fucking awesome. (*To* LISA.) We could go.

AMY. Are you gonna leave?

JOANNE *shrugs*.

When?

JOANNE. In about half an hour if you don't get that fucking
fire started. What we meant to do with two twigs.

AMY. Couldn't find any more.

JOANNE. Up here? All these trees? Go back and have a look.

AMY. It's dead dark.

JOANNE. Scared are you?

AMY. No.

Can't we use the stove?

JOANNE. No, we need a fire, like on *Bear Grylls*, like you said.

We ain't using the sleeping bags.

It's Lisa's party. We want her to be warm, don't we?

LISA. I'm alright.

JOANNE. Go on. Take the torch.

AMY *goes off into the night.*

JOANNE *and* LISA *stand in silence.* JOANNE *gets a piece of cake, pulls the wet bit off and eats it.*

S'good cake actually.

LISA. Yeah?

JOANNE. Yeah. Bit wet but. Proper good actually.

She cracks me up. Magic candles.

We have a right laugh, at the chippy.

LISA. Good.

JOANNE. And we went down Foxy the other day. The wood bit. Didn't see no flashers though.

And town, we went town. (*Gesturing to birthday stuff.*) To get this stuff. So. Was a laugh.

Seen your mum?

LISA. Once.

JOANNE. She alright?

LISA. Same.

JOANNE. Still with

LISA. Yeah.

JOANNE. TJ brought me up here, y'know? When I first met him. Me and Sharon. Brought us up here in his car. We all sat out on the bonnet, looking up at the sky. Watching the stars. He showed us the plough. And Orion's Belt. S'there, look. Can you see it?

LISA. What?

JOANNE. Just like a little row of stars. There, look. Looks like a belt.

I don't really get it. Fuck knows who Orion is. But that's what it's called.

Said to TJ, if I ever have a kid, I'm gonna call it Orion.

LISA. Is anyone coming, Joanne?

JOANNE. No.
No one's coming.

LISA. Cos I've been expecting it. Every day, I've been

JOANNE. No one's coming. S'just us.

I swear.

What?

Just wanted to

see you.

D'ya like your present then, or what?

LISA. Yeah.

I wanted one.

JOANNE. Did you?

LISA. Yeah.

JOANNE. Did you ask Pam?

LISA. She doesn't really like Primark.

JOANNE. Fucking sewing bee, is she?

LISA. Nah. She likes other shops.

JOANNE. What's wrong with Primark?

LISA. She said they use child slaves to sew stuff.

JOANNE. Filled a fucking bag for a tenner last week. Cheers, child slaves.

LISA. All my stuff's from there.

JOANNE. Yeah, cos we always went, didn't we?

LISA. Yeah.

JOANNE. Remember that day we went and chose outfits for each other to try on. You got me in that old-woman dress.

LISA. You got me in that slut dress with all the cut-outs.

JOANNE. Least it was actually in fashion. And we went that place, where the fish bite all the scabby skin off your feet. Oh my God!

LISA. What? It tickled!

JOANNE. You were squirming all over.

LISA. The woman was well pissed off.

JOANNE. Never said nothing though, did she? Cos I give her that look, like, back off with your evil eyes.

LISA. Looked like we'd had a water fight.

JOANNE. She was scraping fish up off the floor for half an hour.

LISA. That was the day we went to watch *Frozen*.

JOANNE. Yeah. I know.

LISA. Only time you ever turned your phone off. Just sat, dead quiet, watching that. Like everything else stopped.

JOANNE. We had a laugh though, din't we?

LISA. Sometimes, yeah.

JOANNE. Sometimes? A lot of times.

Best days, they were.

Bet it's nothing like that now, is it? With No-Primark-Pam and her fucking Keep-Calm-Cult.

LISA. She's nice.

JOANNE. What and Pete the fucking potato-head.

LISA. You've never seen him.

JOANNE. You said it's weird when he pulls his Ed Sheeran shit.

LISA. It's alright.

JOANNE. What does he do? Like every day? How does he, like, talk to you and that?

LISA. Just like, I don't know, sort of like a teacher I s'pose. Like a friendly teacher.

JOANNE. Never met one of them. Int it weird?

LISA. It's alright.

JOANNE. I mean, like. Is he all like 'Good morning. Beautiful day. How's school?'

LISA. Bit.

JOANNE. Don't it break you?

LISA. Bit.

JOANNE. D'ya have to call him Dad?

LISA. No!

I tried to kiss him.

JOANNE. What? Pete?

LISA. Yeah.

It was just me and him. He was playing guitar.

He sits dead close. And you're supposed to know where to look.

JOANNE. So what?

LISA. So I just started dancing.

JOANNE. No shit? What did he do?

LISA. He stopped.

JOANNE. Then what?

LISA. He just stood looking at me. Dead awkward.
   So I kissed him.

JOANNE. Told you he was dirty.

LISA. He pushed me off.

JOANNE. Did he tell her?

LISA. Yeah. We had to have a meeting. I'm not allowed on my own with him.

JOANNE. But they're letting you stay.

LISA. Yeah.

JOANNE. Sounds weird. I wouldn't like it.

LISA. S'alright. Ain't that bad.

JOANNE. S'not like scabby-feet-fish and vodka on Springy Park though, is it?

LISA. It's not like the chip shop, no.

JOANNE. Don't have to go the chip shop.

We could go somewhere else.

LISA. What?

JOANNE. Get away.

Just us.

LISA. You can't leave.

JOANNE. Can do what I want.

LISA. You wouldn't though.

JOANNE. If I did though.

LISA. What?

JOANNE. If I did.

LISA. What?

JOANNE. Would you?

LISA. I can't.

JOANNE. Why?

LISA. Just cos… Pam and that.

JOANNE. What about her?

LISA. She's alright.

JOANNE. Does she know about me?

LISA. What about you?

JOANNE. Just that I'm your best mate. That we was best mates.

LISA. Can't remember. Yeah. Prob'ly.

JOANNE. Cos she never said.

LISA. What?

> JOANNE *throws another present at* LISA.

> What d'ya mean she never / said

JOANNE. Open it.

> LISA *opens the present. It's a moth-eaten stuffed toy.*

LISA. How'd ya get it?

JOANNE. Pam give it me.

LISA. What?

JOANNE. I come round, the other day. Told her we were gonna do a birthday party for you.

LISA. What and she gave you / this?

JOANNE. Yeah. Said if you're gonna be away for the night you'll need Bluie. Said stay out as long as you want.

LISA. Pam did?

JOANNE. Yeah.

LISA. Did you tell her anything?

JOANNE. 'Bout what? As if. Nice room by the way. Not big? It's fucking massive.

> You haven't even asked how I found you.

LISA. How?

JOANNE. Facebook.

LISA. I'm not on Facebook.

JOANNE. Put a status on. MISSING. Thirteen-year-old girl. Put this photo of you, last year. In that Topshop dress. No one shared it. Not one person. So I changed it. MISSING. My beautiful sister. Thirteen. Last seen going to school. Disappeared from the street in broad daylight. Every parent's worst nightmare. Tearing the family apart. Put a picture of you in your Tinkerbell pyjamas. Over a thousand shares. All these people from all over.

This woman wrote on it. God squad she was. Told me she'd
seen you on the street. God bless, she says. So I come and sat
there till I seen you. You don't go out much. Fucking 'ell.

LISA. Does anyone else know?

JOANNE. You never even text. To see if I was okay.

To see if I was alive, fuck's sake.

LISA. I wrote you loads of texts.

JOANNE. I never got no texts.

AMY *appears. She's got a few sticks.*

AMY. I heard loads of noises. Like in the grass and that.

JOANNE. Fuck's sake, is that it?

AMY. It's dead dark. Can't see nothing. It's scary.

JOANNE. Bad stuff don't happen in the dark. It's the light you
wanna worry about. (*About the sticks.*) Fucking pitiful that is.

AMY. I couldn't see. And there was all these sounds. Like as if
someone was up there.

JOANNE. Ain't no one up there.

AMY. She can have my sleeping bag. I don't mind.
We got her the onesie. If she put the onesie on, she'd be
alright.

JOANNE. Yeah, put it on.

LISA. I'm alright.

JOANNE. Put it on.

LISA. I'm warm enough.

JOANNE. You're shivering. Put it on, we got it you, let's see it.

AMY. Go on, just try it on.

JOANNE. Come on, Lisa. Or we'll have to make you.

LISA. What?

JOANNE (*to* AMY). Proper ticklish she is.

LISA. Don't.

JOANNE. Can make her do anything if you tickle her.

> AMY *takes the cue and starts tickling* LISA. LISA *reacts dramatically, squirming and bucking*.

AMY. I'll tickle you to death / I'll tickle you till you die.

LISA. Don't, stop it / get off! Don't

JOANNE. Got loads of videos of her being tickled, an't I?

AMY. What's the magic word? / What's the magic word? Not 'Stop'. Guess the magic word.

LISA. Stop. I don't know. Amy? / I don't know. Get off. Get off me.

AMY. That's not the magic word. That's not / the

LISA. Get the fuck off me.

> LISA *pushes* AMY *to the floor.*

AMY. Joanne.

JOANNE. I never got no texts.

LISA. I never sent them.

JOANNE. Camping's shit. Fucking shit idea.
   Where's this tent even from? Cheap piece o'shit.

AMY. My nana lent it us.

JOANNE. Fucking stinks like sour pussy. Is it yours or your nana's?

AMY. What?

JOANNE. Went camping with her, did you?

AMY. Yeah.

JOANNE. And you thought it was dead good, did you?

> AMY *shrugs*.

Describe it.

AMY. Don't know.

JOANNE. Come on. What did you do?

AMY. Sat out watching the stars.

JOANNE. Sounds shit.
  What else?

AMY. Don't know.

JOANNE. Yeah you do.

AMY. I was like eight.

JOANNE. Come on. What did you do?

AMY. Nothing.

JOANNE. What, so you were just sat there like fucking zombies?

AMY. No. I don't know.

JOANNE. What then?

AMY. We played this game.

JOANNE. What game?

AMY. Just this… it's shit. It's –

JOANNE. What game?

AMY. Where you say 'I went to the shop and I bought an apple'
  and then the next person has to say 'a banana' or / a

JOANNE. Why?

AMY. Cos it starts with a B.

JOANNE. What?

AMY. It's just this game.

JOANNE. Cos it starts with a B?

AMY. It's alphabetised. The alphabet. You say / I

JOANNE. I went to the shop and I bought a banana.

AMY. Yeah, if you was B. Or you might be C. It's a game.

JOANNE. I don't get it.

AMY. It's stupid. Doesn't matter.

JOANNE. Yeah it does. I want to play the fucking game. I went
  to the shop and I bought a banana.

AMY. You'd be apple. If you went first. Doesn't matter.

JOANNE. Yeah it fucking does. No wonder they beat the shit out of you. Acting like you know it all. You don't know nothing.

AMY. I do.

JOANNE. Fucking camping.

AMY. We could pack up. Go the chippy.

JOANNE. Wanna see TJ, do you?

AMY *shrugs*.

He's already give us some chips today. Have to give him something.

AMY. What?

JOANNE. Could send him a picture.

AMY. Of what?

JOANNE. Your tits.

AMY. What? No.

JOANNE. Ain't nothing.

AMY. I haven't got any.

JOANNE. TJ ain't bothered. Smaller the better. Show us 'em and we'll say how many out of ten. Won't we, Lise?

AMY. No.

JOANNE. Come on.

AMY. Don't want to.

JOANNE. But you wanna go the chippy, so take your top off and we'll tell you out of ten. Come on.

AMY. I don't want to.

JOANNE. Bet your nana would.

AMY. What?

JOANNE. Let us see her saggy little tits. Where is she now?

AMY. What?

JOANNE. Where's your nana now?

AMY. Home.

JOANNE. Doing what?

AMY (*shrugs*). Watching telly.

JOANNE. Watching telly, what?

AMY *shrugs*.

What's she fucking watching?

AMY. Don't know.

JOANNE. Cosy, is it?

AMY. What?

JOANNE. In your house.

AMY *shrugs*.

Snuggle up do you. Watch telly?

AMY. No.

JOANNE. Why not?

AMY. Cos I'm not a kid.

JOANNE. What's the baby doing?

AMY. Asleep prob'ly.

JOANNE. Why aren't you there, with 'em?

AMY. Cos I'm here.

JOANNE. Why?

AMY. Cos we're mates. Best mates, you said.

JOANNE. Go and get the baby then.

AMY. What?

JOANNE. If we're best mates. You said you can get it any time.
Go and get it.

AMY. Why?

JOANNE. Wanna take it to the chippy. Gotta take something.

AMY. Why?

JOANNE. Cos it's cute. Can show it TJ. You'll look dead grown-up.

AMY. It's asleep.

JOANNE. What, you got a magic fucking eye or something?

AMY. I can't.

JOANNE. So you was lying then?

AMY. No.

JOANNE. Run home then.

AMY. What?

JOANNE. Run home to Nana.

AMY. I can't go. Cos gotta take the tent. You need the tent.

JOANNE. Take the fucking tent then. Stinks. Take it.

AMY. I don't want to. I want to stay here. I wanna go the chippy.

JOANNE. You're fucking derelict.

AMY. I'm not.

JOANNE. Dropped on your head. Makes sense. You don't know nothing.

AMY. I do.

JOANNE. You don't know fuck-all.

AMY. I know Pam didn't let you in.
I know you broke in.

(*To* LISA.) She stole that toy.

JOANNE. So fuck?

AMY. And your pillow.
She sleeps with it.

JOANNE. You'd better shut your fucking mouth.

AMY. I'm sorry. I'm sorry. I din't mean / to

JOANNE. You wanna go the chippy then?

AMY. Yeah.

JOANNE. Do ya?

AMY. Yeah. I'm sorry. / I'm

JOANNE. Go and get the baby and we'll go.
Go on. Fuck off.

AMY *runs*.

LISA. I've gotta get back. Said I'd be back.

JOANNE. Let us have your phone number, then.

LISA. I don't know it.

JOANNE. Just ring me. Then I'll have it.

LISA. I will.

JOANNE. Now.

LISA. Phone's dead. Just died.

JOANNE. Let's have a look.

LISA. I've gotta go.

LISA *goes to walk away.* JOANNE *blocks her.*

JOANNE. We could go Costa. Work it all out.

LISA. Work what out?

JOANNE. I was in there yesterday. Sat in our seats. Just me.
They still do them cookies you like. They're pumpkins at the
minute. Cos Hallowe'en and that.

LISA. Joanne.

JOANNE. I sat in our seats. And there was this kid on this other
table, Connie. Bet she was IVF. Cos they were all over her.
And her mum's got her one of them cookies you like. Only
she's going fucking mental, kicking and screaming cos
she wanted a cupcake.

LISA. It's late.

JOANNE. And her mum's going 'Excuse me, young lady, I beg
    your pardon, I don't expect a scene like that.' Everyone's
    fucking looking but pretending not to. And her mum goes
    'I know you've had a difficult day, darling, but we're all
    tired.' Only Connie's still fucking fruitloop, chucking stuff.

LISA. I've gotta go.

JOANNE. Fucking 'ell, Lisa. Wait will you. I'm telling a
    fucking story, alright. Connie's going skitz. And then her
    mum, right, her mum runs off to get her a fucking cupcake.

    So I goes up to her, Connie, and I sit opposite her, and I hold
    her little hand. And she's silent then. Her eyes are dead wide,
    looking up at me. Just staring up at me. And I get her hand
    and I hold it on the radiator, trap it really hard, fucking
    roasting radiator, and she's crying, cos it's fucking burning.
    And I'm holding it so she can't escape. And suddenly her
    mum comes back and she's going mental, now. She drops the
    tray and grabs my arm and I'm like 'Er, excuse me, young
    lady, I beg your pardon, I don't expect a scene like that.' And
    everyone's staring, not even pretending not to. And I get
    pulled out by a security guard. Two of them. One of them's
    wearing that Lynx, drowning in that fucking Lynx that TJ
    wears, that fucking... He's outside.

LISA. What?

JOANNE. TJ. He's outside.

LISA. Where?

JOANNE. Pam's.

LISA. What?

JOANNE. He's outside. Now. He's waiting for you.

LISA. How'd you know?

JOANNE. Because I told him.

LISA. Why?

JOANNE. Because I promised him. I promised him I'd find you.

    He ain't gonna do nothing. Not now. Not till you get back.
    Might as well, just, might as well wait here.

LISA. ~~What the.~~ I thought we were… Sisters, you said.

JOANNE. We were.

Then you left me in that room.

LISA. You made me go there.

JOANNE. I didn't have no choice.

LISA. You said I didn't have to do no more parties. You promised.

~~JOANNE. I didn't have no choice.~~

LISA. We could've gone to the police. I said we should.

JOANNE. Why didn't you then?

LISA. Cos of you. I didn't have nowhere to go but I never went the police.

JOANNE. What did the texts say?

LISA. What?

JOANNE. You said you wrote me texts.

LISA. They said I hate you.

JOANNE. So why didn't you send them then?

LISA. Cos I didn't want you finding me.

JOANNE. Give us your phone.

LISA. No.

JOANNE. I said give me your fucking phone.

JOANNE *wrestles* LISA*'s phone from her. The screen is locked.*

What's the code?

LISA. Don't.

JOANNE. Tell me the fucking code.

LISA. 1, 3, 0, 6.

JOANNE. 13, 06. That's my birthday.

LISA *shrugs*.

Drafts.

Joanne:

We went to a carnival. Colours everywhere and these smells of cooking and fireworks and cold air. And I wanted

You wanted what?

LISA. Give it back.

JOANNE. Joanne:

This lad Jake asked me out. And I let him fuck me in his bedroom cos I wanted to see what it would be like. Only it was slow and empty and like ants on your skin.

Joanne:

Pete plays guitar, and he sits proper close, and you're meant to know where to look.

All the things you can't tell no one else.

LISA. Why did you scream?

JOANNE. What?

LISA. At the B&B. When I was trying to get out that room. When I was trying to escape.

JOANNE. What do you mean?

LISA. I couldn't breathe. I was so scared they were gonna kill me if they caught me. And you screamed.

Fucking nine of 'em. You never told me there'd be nine. Cut all my front open on the window trying to escape, and you fucking screamed so they'd see me.

Sisters don't do the shit you do, Joanne.

JOANNE. So why did you come here then? Tonight?

LISA. You said you was gonna burn Pam's face off.

JOANNE. Before that. You had your scarf on soon as you saw me.

LISA. Cos I was scared.

JOANNE. You ain't scared of me, Lisa.

LISA. I keep searching online, you know.

JOANNE. You won't find nothing.

LISA. Sometimes I spend hours. All this fucked-up shit and I'm looking through it for my face. Cos one day someone at school'll see. Or when I'm older, I'll have a kid and she'll see.

JOANNE. I wouldn't post 'em.

LISA. ~~TJ might.~~

JOANNE. ~~TJ ain't got 'em.~~

LISA. Delete them then.

Delete them. Why haven't you deleted them?

Do you watch them?

JOANNE. No.

No, I don't fucking watch them.

LISA. I've gotta go.

Suddenly JOANNE *grabs* LISA *by the hair and pulls her head back.* LISA *tries not to react.* JOANNE *clenches her fist and holds it as though she is going to punch* LISA *in the face. They stare at each other. Instead of punching* LISA, JOANNE *grabs her neck with her free hand, as if she will strangle her. She stares at* LISA*'s face. Then she kisses her on the lips. Then she slaps her, really hard.*

JOANNE. I screamed so you could get away.

LISA. What?

JOANNE. They was about to catch you sliding out the window. So I screamed.

So they'd have to shut me up first.

~~Moshi put his fist in my mouth.~~

LISA. Liar.

JOANNE. What the fuck do you know? You was halfway down the motorway.

I screamed so you could get away.

~~Moshi put his fist in my mouth.~~

Then they all got on me, din't they? All of 'em. ~~Cos I was on my own, wan't I?~~

The B&B woman came to the door. Came knocking and they stopped then, dead still. Like fucking animals when you catch 'em in the dark.

~~I could see her feet, the shadow of her feet, in that crack of light.~~ I was waiting for her to come in. Open the door with one of them magic keys. But she didn't. ~~She just told them to keep the noise down and went away.~~

LISA. What did they do?

JOANNE. Everything.

Could see my insides. Ain't bothered, but…

Kept expecting the police to turn up.

LISA. You told me to never go to the police. You said they'd kill us if we ever went.

JOANNE. I went once.

LISA. What?

JOANNE. Before. When I was thirteen. Before I met you.

LISA. You never.

JOANNE. I was drunk. I was kicking off.

LISA. Liar.

What did they say then?

JOANNE. They said 'Off the record, there are thirteen-year-old girls and there are thirteen-year-old girls, if you know what I mean.'

I told a teacher as well. Didn't tell her names, didn't tell her who but…

She fucking cried.

LISA. Then what?

JOANNE. Then she found me sucking three lads off in the school toilet and expelled me. Sat in Asda every day for a week on this chair watching everyone buy all their stuff. Security man kept moving me on.

LISA. Didn't no one come looking for you?

JOANNE. Ain't no one looking for people like me.

He used to say I was cute. But not like a baby cute.

None of them want me now. They tell him not to send me. Only way he wants me now is if I find you. If I get Amy. And more. He wants more.

You were always asking to go the chippy.

I wasn't gonna text him. I wasn't gonna tell.

LISA. So why did you?

JOANNE. What else am I gonna do? If he knew I'd seen you, he'd kill me. Worse.

I had it all planned out, y'know. The party and that.

Was gonna give you the onesie, then these…

JOANNE *pulls out some train tickets from her pocket.*

LISA. Train tickets.

JOANNE. To Skeggie, then Bluie, to put in your bag. Then we'd go.

LISA. To do the Disney thing?

JOANNE *shrugs.*

Does Sharon really do that?

JOANNE. ~~Yeah.~~
  No.
  ~~But she does live in Skegness. She has got her own room.~~

LISA. Have you been?

JOANNE. No. But we could go now. Walk down the tracks to the station. I've got some money. Been saving up. Stuff TJ gives me.

LISA. And do what?

JOANNE. See the sea.

  Work in a café or summat. There's loads of cafés.

LISA. I'm gonna do my GCSEs.

JOANNE. Why?

LISA. Be a nurse. Wanna help people.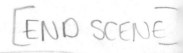

JOANNE. I know you want what everyone wants. A family. A home. But you'll never have it. Cos of what's inside you.

  ~~It'll be a new start. We can do whatever we want.~~

  You can tell me all the shit you can't tell no one else. Any time, you can tell me. ~~All the dark stuff eating you up. And I'll understand, won't I? I'll get it.~~

  ~~JOANNE *holds the train tickets out.*~~

  ~~There's loads of pubs there. Dead cheap. And bars. Not even strict.~~
  ~~And they've got donkeys. On the beach. Fucking donkeys. Proper cute. And them two-pee machines, like on TV, like on that *Tipping Point*.~~

LISA. Ain't never seen the sea.

JOANNE. It's amazing.

LISA. When did you go the sea?

JOANNE. I ain't, but. It is.

  Sound of a train coming.

  Hear that?

  Gotta stay on, long as you dare.

First one to jump off has to swim in the sea naked.

Pretend you're in the Olympics. On the beam. Pretend you're Darcy in *Strictly*. Bend and stretch. S'like you're on fire! It's like every bit of you's electric. Is that it, Lise? Is that what you said?

LISA. Like you're made of electric.

Suddenly LISA *runs up to the tracks.* JOANNE *follows her. The train is close.*

Like sparks shooting out of you.

JOANNE. Like you're alive!

LISA/JOANNE (*together, by coincidence, takes them by surprise*). Like you're invincible!

JOANNE. One

Don't jump off, don't you dare jump off

LISA/JOANNE. Two

Three, juuuuuuummmmmp!

The train races past. JOANNE *helps* LISA *up and they start to leave.*

Suddenly AMY *appears. She's put her hair up. She has a backpack on her back.*

AMY. Joanne! Lisa! Wait. Wait!

JOANNE. Where's the baby?

AMY. She was asleep. She / was

JOANNE. Told you.

AMY. I've got something better.

JOANNE. We've gotta go.

AMY. Where?

JOANNE. Gotta walk Lisa back. It's cold.

AMY. I've got something. A surprise. To keep us warm.

JOANNE. We ain't stopping out no more.

AMY. I'll walk with you.

JOANNE. No.

AMY. We could go the chippy, then. All of us.

JOANNE. Told you. We can't.

> AMY *runs up to the railway track. She takes her bag off her back.*

AMY. Wait. I couldn't get the baby, so I thought… and I knew you wanted to go the chippy, only we couldn't, you said we couldn't, and I know you said I was a kid, and I'm not, so I thought…

> AMY *pulls out chips wrapped in paper.*

JOANNE. What?

AMY. Chips. And I got a fritter for you, Joanne, cos I know they're your favourite. TJ said / it's

LISA. TJ's at the chippy?

AMY. I told him we were camping. He said we must be mental. He said it's way too cold for camping. I said that's what you said, Joanne.

LISA (*to* JOANNE). Does he know about me, or not?

AMY. They're the best chips, from TJ's. He said we can go back any time and then, when I said –

LISA. Joanne?

JOANNE. Did you tell him about Lisa?

AMY. What about Lisa?

LISA. Did you tell him I'm up here?

JOANNE. Did you tell him I found her? Did you?

AMY. You said it was a secret.

JOANNE. So you didn't?

AMY. No.

JOANNE. Swear?

AMY. I swear.

JOANNE. We can still leave, Lisa. If we go now.

AMY. What?

JOANNE. If we stay on the tracks, we can just walk to the station, it's not far.

He doesn't know. He doesn't know nothing.

AMY. We can go back to the chippy. It's alright. I've sorted it.

I give him a picture. Like you told me.

He said he'll send a taxi.

JOANNE (*to* LISA). We could be there tomorrow. Just us two.

Like before. Best days they were.

LISA. They were the worst fucking days of my life, Joanne.

JOANNE (*to* AMY). I told you to never go to the chippy without me. Didn't I? Didn't I tell you? Never go to the fucking chippy without me?

JOANNE lays into AMY, *violently beating her.* LISA *pulls* JOANNE *away and holds her from behind.*

LISA. She's a fucking baby, Joanne.

JOANNE. I was.

LISA *holds* JOANNE *awkwardly. Neither wants it to end.*

Who lives there d'ya reckon?

The little one, there.

LISA. I don't know.

JOANNE. with two windows, there. / That one.

LISA. I don't know, Joanne.

JOANNE shrugs LISA *off her back.*

JOANNE. Go on then.

LISA. What?

JOANNE. Take her with you, will you?

LISA. She needs help.

JOANNE. You wanna help people, remember.
She's got her nana, han't she?
Go with her, Amy.

LISA. What you gonna do?

JOANNE. Got the train tickets, haven't I? I'll go and see
Sharon. She keeps asking me, anyway.

Go on then.

LISA and AMY start to leave.

Walk along the train tracks.

*LISA and AMY go up to the track together. JOANNE
doesn't look back to watch them.*

LISA. Come with us.

JOANNE. Wanna tidy this up. Wanna take it with me.

LISA. We've gotta go.

JOANNE. So go.

LISA and AMY start to walk away.

LISA. Joanne.

JOANNE. What?

LISA. It's Elsie.

JOANNE. What?

LISA. In the house with two windows. Elsie.

JOANNE. Just Elsie?

LISA. Yeah.

JOANNE. What's she like?

LISA. Proper old.

Paper for skin, like see-through skin.

And little hands. Blue veins creeping all over them, like a map. Twiglets for fingers. And eyelids like hoods. Little hoods that open and close like clockwork.

JOANNE. What does she do, Elsie?

LISA. She just waits for the grandkids to visit. Cos they're the best days.

AMY and LISA disappear. JOANNE is alone. LISA has left all the presents.

We hear the sound of a car coming. The headlights shine through trees and on to JOANNE . The engine stops.

JOANNE*'s phone beeps.*

Lights out.

A Nick Hern Book

All the Little Lights first published in Great Britain in 2017 as a paperback original by Nick Hern Books Limited, The Glasshouse, 49a Goldhawk Road, London W12 8QP, in association with Fifth Word

All the Little Lights copyright © 2017 Jane Upton

Jane Upton has asserted her moral right to be identified as the author of this work

Designed and typeset by Nick Hern Books, London
Printed in the UK by Mimeo Ltd, Huntingdon, Cambridgeshire PE29 6XX

A CIP catalogue record for this book is available from the British Library

ISBN   978 1 84842 635 1